Presented To

_____

Presented By

_____

Date

_____

PROVERBS FOR LIFE™
FOR LIFE™
for
Graduates

inspirio™

Proverbs for Life™ for Graduates
ISBN 0-310-80192-3

Copyright © 2004 by GRQ Ink, Inc.
Franklin, Tennessee 37067
"Proverbs for Life" is a trademark owned by GRQ, Inc.

Published by Inspirio™, The gift group of Zondervan
5300 Patterson Avenue, SE
Grand Rapids, Michigan 49530

Requests for information should be addressed to:
Inspirio™, The gift group of Zondervan
Grand Rapids, Michigan 49530
http://www.inspiriogifts.com

Compiler: Lila Empson
Associate Editor: Janice Jacobson
Project Manager: Tom Dean
Credit Line: Manuscript written by Mark Weising in conjunction with
   Snapdragon Editorial Group, Inc.
Design: Whisner Design Group

03 04 05/HK/ 4 3 2 1

Wisdom is sweet

to your soul;

if you find it,

there is a future hope

for you.

Proverbs 24:14 niv

Contents

Introduction

The book of Proverbs contains the timeless wisdom each person needs to live a happy, healthy, well-balanced life—each entry teaching a practical principle designed to encourage good choices and positive problem solving.

Proverbs for Life™ for Graduates takes those valuable principles and applies them to the issues you care about most—such as family, health, peace, and commitment. As you read through these pages, may you find the practical answers—God's answers—to the questions you are asking.

Listen to advice and accept instruction, and in the end you will be wise.

— Proverbs 19:20 NIV

Seeking the Future

G**OD, IF** T**HY WILL BE SO,**

E**NRICH THE TIME TO COME WITH**

S**MOOTH-FACED PEACE,**

W**ITH SMILING PLENTY AND**

F**AIR PROSPEROUS DAYS!**

W**ILLIAM** S**HAKESPEARE**

The Road Ahead

Let reverence for the LORD be the concern of your life. If it is, you have a bright future.

~ *Proverbs* 23:17–18 GNT

Even though school isn't easy, it is usually predictable. At the first class, most teachers hand out a syllabus detailing what you can expect from the semester ahead—exam dates, paper and project requirements, and reading assignments. But life after school has more unknowns and is more difficult to anticipate.

When you encounter uncertainty about the future, it's good to know that God holds your future in his hands. He has already seen it and paved the road ahead of you. He has promised in his Word to see you safely along each step of the way. All he asks is that you trust him—that you take one step at a time. He will be there to provide wisdom and discernment and confidence enough for each additional step.

It is possible to greet the future with a clear sense of vision. Let God be your navigator, and you will reach your destination right on time.

> Never be afraid to trust an unknown future to a known God.
>
> Corrie ten Boom

꩜ Stepping out of the structured lifestyle you were used to at school into the wide world of choices and opportunities can seem almost like a free fall. But it really isn't. As you take the steps you know to take each day, God will provide the vision and guidance you need for each tomorrow. He will show you the way in, around, over, or through every obstacle. And he will point out opportunities as well. You can trust him for each step.

꩜ TRY THIS: *As you spend your daily quiet time with God, ask him to bless the steps that are clearly before you today. Record those steps — things like brainstorming an idea with a friend, reading a certain passage in the Bible, working on your résumé, or asking someone for advice. Take the steps you know today, and God will reveal the steps for tomorrow.*

OH LORD OUR GOD; THERE IS NO ONE LIKE YOU! YOU HAVE MADE MANY WONDERFUL PLANS FOR US.

PSALM 40:5 GNT

WISDOM IS GOOD FOR THE SOUL. GET WISDOM AND YOU HAVE A BRIGHT FUTURE.

PROVERBS 24:14 GNT

I don't know what the future holds, but I know who holds the future.

AUTHOR UNKNOWN

11

Following Your Inner Calm

A peaceful heart gives life to the body.

~ Proverbs 14:30 NIrV

Darin was sure that once he had his diploma in hand he'd know exactly what God wanted him to do. But three weeks after graduation, he still wasn't sure. He found himself sitting at the kitchen table wondering which option to pursue. He had three solid job offers, a ministry opportunity, and a letter of acceptance from a graduate program.

He had many good things to choose from, but Darin wanted more—he wanted God's best. Darin asked God to make the right choice evident to him. "Show me which path you want me to take, Lord, and I will pursue it with all my strength."

Darin prayed diligently. As he did, one job offer began to stand out in his mind. As he sought to learn more about it and to evaluate it more closely, he felt a deep sense of peace sweep over him, bringing with it a sense of inner calm assurance. Darin felt certain he had heard from God.

꧁ The Bible calls Jesus Christ the Prince of Peace because he brought peace to the relationship between God and humanity. He also brings peace to your heart as you pursue his will for your life. Deep, lasting peace is a sign of his presence and his approval. It is your green light, the signal that you are moving in the right direction to fulfill his purposes for you.

꧁ TRY THIS: *On a note card, write out Philippians 4:6–7, "Do not worry about anything, but in everything by prayer and supplication with thanksgiving let your requests be made known to God. And the peace of God, which surpasses all understanding, will guard your hearts and your minds in Christ Jesus" (NIV). Read this scripture each day for reassurance.*

DEPART FROM EVIL AND DO GOOD; SEEK PEACE, AND PURSUE IT.

PSALM 34:14 NRSV

WISDOM'S WAYS ARE WAYS OF PLEASANTNESS, AND ALL HER PATHS ARE PEACE.

PROVERBS 3:17 NRSV

Who except God can give you peace? Has the world ever been able to satisfy the heart?

GERARD MAJELLA

Excellence

Be the duties great or small,
though you falter, often fall,
He will hear when e'er you call.

Do your best!

Look to God in all you do,
For some work He's planned for you,
And be faithful, loyal, true.

Do your best!

Author Unknown

*Hands that work hard
will rule.*

~ *Proverbs* 12:24 NIrV

*If there is any
excellence and if there
is anything worthy of
praise, think about these
things.*

~ *Philippians* 4:8 NRSV

A REPUTATION FOR
EXCELLENCE WILL
TAKE YOU WHERE
THE MEDIOCRE
ONLY DREAM
OF GOING.

ANDREA GARNEY

Pursuing Your Dreams

The desire of the righteous will be granted.

~ *Proverbs 10:24* NRSV

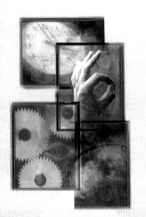

> When your heart is in your dream, no request is too extreme.
>
> Jiminy Cricket

Janice hurled her mortarboard cap in the air with great enthusiasm. Finally, the first stage of her plan to become a neurosurgeon was complete. She knew she still had a long journey ahead of her, but she had no doubt that she would make it.

When Janice was fifteen years old, a local neurosurgeon had visited her high school. A dream was born in her heart that day as she listened to him describe the gifts needed to succeed in the field and tell stories of cases where his skills had changed lives. That night she had shared her growing excitement with God and asked him to keep her in the path of his perfect will.

After that, Janice's dream had taken a firm grip on her thinking. With it came the assurance that God would see her through every step of the way. Now, Step One was complete and Step Two was beckoning.

God wants to help you identify those ambitions that are in accordance with his will and purpose for your life, because they will bring you the greatest degree of success and personal fulfillment. Ask God to remove those dreams that serve only as distractions. Then ask him to firmly establish those dreams that he has placed in your heart. You will soon find yourself losing interest in some things, while others become stronger and more established in your thinking.

Try this: List your three strongest aspirations. Don't concern yourself with how large, or seemingly unlikely they might be. For one week, pray over the first item on your list. The second week, pray over the second, and so on until you have spent a week praying over each ambition. Ask God to remove or establish each one in your heart.

THE PATH OF THE RIGHTEOUS IS LIKE THE LIGHT OF DAWN, WHICH SHINES BRIGHTER AND BRIGHTER UNTIL FULL DAY.

PROVERBS 4:18 NRSV

COMMIT TO THE LORD WHATEVER YOU DO, AND YOUR PLANS WILL SUCCEED.

PROVERBS 16:3 NIV

Reach high, for stars lie hidden in your soul. Dream deep, for every dream precedes the goal.

PAMELA STARR

Knowing Where You're Going

The mind of man plans his way, but the LORD directs his steps.

~ *Proverbs 16:9* NASB

From the age of eight, Emily had dreamed of becoming a concert pianist, and in the years following she mapped out her life to accomplish that one goal. With her natural ability and long hours of practice, she gained admittance into the most prestigious music school in the country.

Shortly after graduation, however, Emily began feeling pain whenever she played. A specialist diagnosed her with a rare form of tendonitis. For the first time in her life, Emily no longer had a clear plan. As she sought God in prayer, all she could say was, "Help me, Lord, I don't know where I'm going."

God soon answered Emily's prayer when an acquaintance asked her to give her daughter piano lessons. Emily found teaching to be a rewarding experience, and one that provided far less stress than playing concerts. She soon began taking on more students. As Emily thanked God for answering her prayer, she decided to worry less about planning in the future and more about seeking his will.

As a student, you probably learned good planning techniques that will help you succeed in life after graduation. A good plan will help you know which goals to pursue and will give you the motivation to get there. However, be sure to look with anticipation for the surprises along the way. Be flexible and allow yourself to change your plans when God puts an interesting challenge in your path. You will find that his plans are always better than those you had in mind.

Try this: *Plan a short trip to somewhere you've never been. Consult a road map, but don't plan your activities. Ask God to bless your trip and help you to see the things around you that you normally wouldn't notice. Stop and enjoy interesting roadside attractions. Trust in God's plan for your destination.*

You ought to say, "If it is the Lord's will, we will live and do this or that."

James 4:15 NIV

Whether you turn to the right or to the left, your ears will hear a voice behind you, saying, "This is the way; walk in it."

Isaiah 30:21 NIV

The future is as bright as the promises of God.

Adoniram Judson

Asking and Receiving

The LORD heareth the prayer of the righteous.

— *Proverbs* 15:29 KJV

HE WHO HAS
LEARNED TO PRAY
HAS LEARNED THE
GREATEST SECRET
OF A HOLY AND
A HAPPY LIFE.

WILLIAM LAW

After graduating from a university in his hometown, Sal was recruited by an engineering company in another state. He was excited about the prospect of being out on his own and doing things the way he wanted. Sal's mind was filled with thoughts about everything he could experience in another location. But he also knew there was a lot he didn't know, and he needed some guidance, God's guidance.

Sal had grown up praying. He had always prayed before meals, in church, before he went to sleep, whenever he needed God's help. Now prayer was more important than ever to him. Sal found himself talking to God on the way to work in the morning and whispering a prayer before making a decision on the job site.

As Sal began to make new friends and become more confident at work, he continued to talk to God more and more. Prayer had become a living reality for him.

Prayer is direct access to God, who transcends time and distance and obstacles. Far more than a life preserver to be used only in times of trouble, it is sweet fellowship for every moment of the day. If you've known prayer only as a religious ritual or last-ditch solution to a problem, open your heart to God and try talking to him about the everyday things that happen in your life. Every time you feel like talking, God is listening.

TRY THIS: *The next time you're alone—at home, at work, in your car, wherever—strike up a conversation with God. Talk to him about your concerns, your triumphs, your day. Speak to him just as you would a close friend. Your conversation can be as long or as short as you like.*

THE PRAYER OF A RIGHTEOUS MAN IS POWERFUL AND EFFECTIVE.

JAMES 5:16 NIV

THE PRAYER OF THE UPRIGHT IS GOD'S DELIGHT.

PROVERBS 15:8 KJV

To pray with understanding is to pray as being instructed by the Spirit in the understanding of the want of those things which the soul is to pray for.

JOHN BUNYAN

Life and Longing

The hope of the righteous ends in gladness.

— *Proverbs 10:28* NRSV

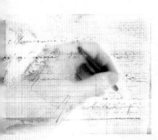

If you do not hope you will never discover what is beyond your hopes.

Clement of Alexandria

After high-school graduation, you may be one of the thousands of young adults who enroll in various colleges across the country. When classes begin, you'll focus your attention on learning the material, writing papers, studying for exams, and taking progressively appropriate courses. Why would you do that? Because you are hoping that the hard work you put in will pay off big in the future.

Living a Christian life also requires a steady focus and consistent commitment. But your hope in Christ has an even greater payoff—the fulfillment of God's wonderful promises for this life and also for the life to come. The hope you place in God will never fail you. He will always be there to look out for you, to help you find solutions, and to help you overcome whatever obstacles lie between you and your achievements. That's a promise you can depend on.

꧂ It's a great privilege to live your life for God and put your trust in someone other than yourself. But sometimes, it may be hard for you to understand why he is leading you in a particular direction or allowing you to struggle through a problematic situation. Hope means looking beyond the present and believing that God always has a plan and purpose for your life. So persevere. The hope of the righteous truly ends in gladness.

꧂ TRY THIS: *Write down three things that you are working toward in the future. Sign and date the paper, seal it in an envelope, and place it in your Bible. Open it at least three years from now and determine if you reached your goals. How have your hopes and commitment changed over time?*

HOPE DOES NOT DISAPPOINT US, BECAUSE GOD HAS POURED OUT HIS LOVE INTO OUR HEARTS BY THE HOLY SPIRIT, WHOM HE HAS GIVEN US.

ROMANS 5:5 NIV

THE DESIRE OF THE RIGHTEOUS ENDS ONLY IN GOOD.

PROVERBS 11:23 NIV

I place no hope in my strength, nor in my works: but all my confidence is in God my protector, who never abandons those who have put all their hope and thought in him.

FRANÇOIS RABELAIS

Endurance

When running in the race of life,
And faced with all its toil and strife,
It may seem that the thing to do
Is give up running halfway through.
But that is when you need to pray
And ask the Lord for strength this day,
To run the race until it's done
And claim the victory you have won.

Edward Ellis

Let your eyes look straight ahead. Keep looking right in front of you.

~ *Proverbs 4:25 NIrV*

Do you not know that those who run in a race all run, but only one receives the prize? Run in such a way that you may win.

~ *1 Corinthians 9:24 NASB*

ENDURANCE IS THE CROWNING QUALITY, AND PATIENCE ALL THE PASSION OF GREAT HEARTS.

JAMES RUSSELL LOWELL

Working Hard

The longings of people who work hard are completely satisfied.

~ *Proverbs 13:4 NIrV*

From a young age, Sarah knew she enjoyed helping people. After graduating from high school, she investigated several possible courses of study and decided to pursue a degree in social work.

Sarah soon realized that becoming a social worker was not an easy task. In addition to taking difficult classes and holding down a part-time job, Sarah served as an intern at various local agencies while working on her bachelor's degree. She then went on to obtain her master's degree, after which she studied for months to pass two state licensing exams.

Despite the difficulty of her task, Sarah knew that God was calling her into this profession. She thanked him for giving her the longing to help others and the strength to pursue her goal diligently. Graduation was a real victory, and Sarah enjoyed every moment of it. At the same time, she knew that more hard work (and more fulfillment) lay in the path ahead.

Sometimes the work involved in reaching your goals and following the path that God has laid out for you may seem overwhelming, and you may have to deal with discouragement and fatigue along the way. In these situations it is important to remember that God will reward your faithfulness and diligence. Try to focus on the prize waiting for you at the finish line, and ask God to give you the strength and determination to the stay the course.

Try this: *Choose two things you need to get done but have been putting off. Write down specific things you need to do to accomplish them. Schedule a one-hour block of time to work on each task, and build in a personal reward for finishing each one so that you work progressively toward accomplishing what you desire.*

Jesus said, "My Father is always at his work to this very day, and I, too, am working."

John 5:17 NIV

Hands that don't want to work make you poor. But hands that work hard bring wealth to you.

Proverbs 10:4 NIrV

It is not only prayer that gives God glory, but work.
GERALD MANLEY HOPKINS

Leaning on the Lord

Whoever trusts in the LORD will be enriched.

~ *Proverbs* 28:25 NRSV

Here I pause in my sojourning, giving thanks for having come, come to trust, at every turning, God will guide me safely home.

Robert Robinson

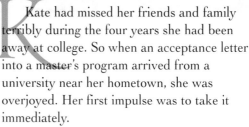

Kate had missed her friends and family terribly during the four years she had been away at college. So when an acceptance letter into a master's program arrived from a university near her hometown, she was overjoyed. Her first impulse was to take it immediately.

Kate prayed about the decision with some friends at church. The more she prayed, the more convinced she was that God was telling her to stay put for a while. Kate was confused—she had talked to God frequently during the past four years about her homesickness. But she had always trusted in God and knew in her heart that this time would be no different.

A few months later God brought a newcomer named Paul into church and into Kate's life. The two began dating, and a year later they were married. As Kate looked back on her decision to stay, she thanked God for giving her the confidence to trust in him and wait for what he had planned.

In the Bible, there are many examples of people who trusted God even when they didn't understand why he was leading them in a certain direction. Abraham, for example, was asked to leave the place where he had lived all his life, the place where all his relatives and his wife's relatives resided, to follow God to an unknown destination. Abraham placed his trust in God and became the father of a new nation, whose offspring occupied a bountiful land given to them by God.

Jesus said, "Do not let your hearts be troubled. Trust in God; trust also in me."

John 14:1 NIV

Try this: *This week, try to think of two or three times when you trusted God and he proved his faithfulness to you. Write them down as they come to you, and keep the list on your bathroom mirror where you can be reminded often that God is faithful and true to his word.*

Trust in the Lord with all your heart; and lean not on your own understanding.

Proverbs 3:5 NIV

Conquer we must when our cause it is just, and this be our motto, in God is our trust!

Francis Scott Key

Words Smartly Spoken

Those who guard their mouths preserve their lives.

— *Proverbs 13:3* NRSV

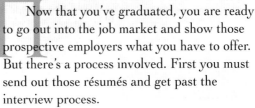

SPEAK CLEARLY,
IF YOU SPEAK AT
ALL; CARVE EVERY
WORD BEFORE
YOU LET IT FALL.

OLIVER WENDALL
HOLMES SR.

Now that you've graduated, you are ready to go out into the job market and show those prospective employers what you have to offer. But there's a process involved. First you must send out those résumés and get past the interview process.

Job interviews are tricky because you must convince an employer in a short period of time that you are the best person for the job. You must carefully choose your words to show that you are a dedicated and hard-working individual. You must guard against saying things that would place your qualifications in doubt.

God wants you to guard your speech in all your interactions in much the same way you would in a job interview. If you wouldn't fly off the handle and make chiding remarks in an interview with strangers, then you shouldn't do so in your conversations with the people you really care about. Remember, you are representing God's company.

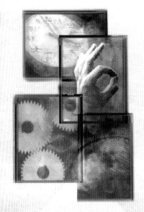

The words you speak have the power to hurt and to heal, to tear down and to build up. What an incredible responsibility God has given you to use your words wisely and effectively. Take the time and effort necessary to ensure that your words are truthful and encouraging. Lace them with hope for the sake of those who feel hopeless. Sprinkle them with wisdom for those who need guidance. Energize them with love for those who have not known love. Make your words count.

Try this: *Each morning, determine to give at least three compliments sometime during the day. Look for opportunities in your interactions with friends, family members, or even strangers. When you notice something good, speak out. Keep it up until it becomes a habit and you become an excellent representative of God.*

LISTEN, FOR I HAVE WORTHY THINGS TO SAY; I OPEN MY LIPS TO SPEAK WHAT IS RIGHT.

PROVERBS 8:6 NIV

SET A GUARD OVER MY MOUTH, O LORD; KEEP WATCH OVER THE DOOR OF MY LIPS.

PSALM 141:3 NIV

Always speak the truth — think before you speak.

LEWIS CARROLL

Picking Up the Pieces

Hope deferred makes the heart sick, but a desire fulfilled is a tree of life.

~ *Proverbs 13:12* NRSV

WE LEARN WISDOM FROM FAILURE MUCH MORE THAN FROM SUCCESS. HE WHO NEVER MADE A MISTAKE NEVER MADE A DISCOVERY.

SAMUEL SMILES

It had been two months since graduation. John had received only a few responses to the hundreds of résumés he had sent out, but none looked too promising. He had done well in his graphic design classes and had achieved honors recognition. But it looked like no one was eager to hire a college graduate with no experience.

John was disappointed, but he tried not to let it get him down. Instead, he decided to take it to the Lord. "God, I really believe this is what you want me to do," he prayed. "But if not, show me the job you want me to do and the direction I need to go. I put it into your hands."

Although his situation hadn't changed, John felt as if a burden had been lifted. He was no longer alone in his struggle, for God was right there with him. More disappointments would follow, but John was confident that God was on his side.

The Bible says that if you come to Christ when you are weary and burdened, he will give you rest. All you have to do is surrender control of the situation to him and allow him to lead you in the direction he wants you to take. While disappointment is never easy to accept, it is often a good way to learn the valuable and important lessons that God wants to teach you.

Try this: *Choose a group that offers support and understanding. This might be a Sunday school class, a support group, or a circle of close friends. Find a group on whom you can lean during difficult times and with whom you can rejoice during good times, and learn how to surrender control and leave yourself open to God's leading.*

I CALL TO GOD, THE MOST HIGH, TO GOD, WHO SUPPLIES MY EVERY NEED.

PSALM 57:2 GNT

JESUS SAID, "COME TO ME, ALL WHO ARE WEARY AND HEAVY-LADEN, AND I WILL GIVE YOU REST."

MATTHEW 11:28 NASB

Blest are the pure in heart, for they shall see our God; the secret of the Lord is theirs, their soul is Christ's abode.

JOHN KEBLE

Achievement

When sunset falls upon your day
And business cares are put away,
How do you measure your success—
In terms of wealth or happiness?

If you have eased some others' pain
Or worked to bring them greater gain,
If you have faced the bitter fight
And stood for what you know is right,
Then you shouldn't even have to guess
The day now o'er was a real success.

Author Unknown

The wise inherit honor.

~ *Proverbs 3:35* NIV

I press on toward the goal to win the prize for which God has called me heavenward in Christ Jesus.

~ *Philippians 3:14* NIV

FOUR STEPS TO ACHIEVEMENT:

1. PLAN PURPOSEFULLY.

2. PREPARE PRAYERFULLY.

3. PROCEED POSITIVELY.

4. PURSUE PERSISTENTLY.

WILLIAM A. WARD

Securing Your Way

One who moves too hurriedly misses the way.

~ *Proverbs 19:2 NRSV*

LOOK BEFORE
YOU LEAP; FOR
AS YOU SOW,
YOU ARE LIKELY
TO REAP.

SAMUEL BUTLER

When she graduated from high school, Beth was offered a scholarship at the out-of-state university she desired to attend. The scholarship covered tuition, books, and fees. It covered everything except on-campus housing. Beth decided she would be better off financially if she found a roommate and located an apartment off campus.

But Beth's parents were uneasy about her alternative plan. College would be her first experience in living away from home. They expressed their concern to her that trying to make it on her own and getting used to college at the same time could be too stressful.

At first Beth felt her parents were being overprotective. As she prayed about the decision, however, she wondered whether they might be right after all. Was she ready to be responsible for rent and utility bills? Would she feel safe? Ultimately, Beth agreed with her parents. She belonged in the dorm, regardless of the cost.

Exercising caution means giving careful consideration to a situation to avoid unnecessary risk or danger. It means thinking things through carefully before acting. It means considering the merits of advice given by those who love you. Caution does not mean living in fear, but it does mean living with a healthy respect for unexpected dangers. It is simply taking the time needed to ensure your best possible opportunity for success. Graduation may provide the first opportunity for being on your own. Proceed with caution.

Try this: *When considering an action, ask yourself the following questions: Will this action place me in unnecessary danger? Would it place at risk something I can't afford to lose? Would those who love me approve? If you answer yes to any of those questions, it's a good idea to pray about it and seek advice before acting.*

THE PLANS OF THE DILIGENT LEAD TO PROFIT AS SURELY AS HASTE LEADS TO POVERTY.

PROVERBS 21:5 NIV

BE CAREFUL HOW YOU WALK, NOT AS UNWISE MEN BUT AS WISE, MAKING THE MOST OF YOUR TIME.

EPHESIANS 5:15–16 NASB

Look twice before you leap.
CHARLOTTE BRONTË

Choosing Wisely

Godly people are careful about the friends they choose.
— Proverbs 12:26 NIrV

After graduation, Derek and his close circle of school friends said goodbye and headed off in different directions. They promised to stay close, but soon the phone calls and letters started coming less frequently. Derek missed his buddies, and he began to feel depressed and lonely.

Derek had plenty of opportunities to meet new people and make friends at his new job. But most of the people seemed to be interested only in partying, going to dance clubs, and drinking. Most of them, but not Grady. He was different from the rest.

Grady was just the kind of friend Derek had been seeking. They shared many interests, and together they joined a community softball team and spent time rock climbing at a nearby park. Derek was pleased to discover that Grady also shared his faith in God.

Derek's friendship with Grady grew stronger as the years went by. They both saw their friendship as a lifelong gift from their heavenly Father.

God is the best friend you could ever have. He is loyal and kind, wise and understanding. He loves you deeply and is committed to staying by your side. When you want to talk, he's always ready to listen. God wants to be your friend—the Bible says he does. It says that he created humankind because he longed for companionship. You need never walk alone when you can have the greatest friend of all.

Try this: Initiate a conversation with someone you would like to befriend. Invite that person to attend a sporting event or a movie. Afterward, get to know each other. Talk about your interests, hobbies, and those things you feel strongly about—including your faith in God. You'll soon discover if you share the same values.

A FRIEND LOVES AT ALL TIMES.

PROVERBS 17:17 NIV

TWO ARE BETTER THAN ONE, BECAUSE THEY HAVE A GOOD RETURN FOR THEIR WORK: IF ONE FALLS DOWN, HIS FRIEND CAN HELP HIM UP.

ECCLESIASTES 4:9–10 NIV

Be courteous to all, but intimate with few, and let those few be well tried before you give them your confidence.

GEORGE WASHINGTON

Too Many Wants

The greedy person stirs up strife, but whoever trusts in the LORD will be enriched.

~ *Proverbs* 28:25 NRSV

HONEST POVERTY
LIVES HAPPILY;
ILL-GOTTEN
WEALTH
WORRIES.

ANCIENT PROVERB

The verse in Matthew made Jeff pause and think. Jesus, in his famous Sermon on the Mount, was telling the crowds not to store up earthly treasures, but rather to store up heavenly ones: "For where your treasure is, there your heart will be also."

While in school, Jeff had been pursuing a curriculum that would bring him the greatest of wealth and social status. But since graduation, he had been sensing that God wanted him to realign his priorities. Now, as he sat staring at the passage in Matthew, he realized that he had been following a path of greed rather than a path of blessings through a pursuit of God.

Jeff prayed that he would be able to focus on the things of God's kingdom, rather than of this world. As he placed his trust in God, he began to relax and rest in the fact that God would be providing for his needs.

Having material possessions and status is not inherently wrong or evil. In fact, the Bible states that God often blessed those who followed him with such things. The problem occurs when the love and desire for wealth or status becomes the focus of your life. By constantly chasing after things you may miss the blessings that God wants to bestow on you. True happiness comes from the gifts that God provides.

TRY THIS: *List what makes you feel safe. Is money on your list? Ask yourself, How much money would be enough to assure my security? What would I do if I suddenly lost everything? Think about giving money or volunteering your time to a local charity. Consider what other things will also make you feel secure, and what steps you can take to obtain them.*

WHOEVER LOVES MONEY NEVER HAS MONEY ENOUGH.

ECCLESIASTES 5:10 NIV

STORE UP FOR YOURSELVES TREASURES IN HEAVEN, WHERE NEITHER MOTH NOR RUST CONSUMES AND WHERE THIEVES DO NOT BREAK IN AND STEAL. FOR WHERE YOUR TREASURE IS, THERE YOUR HEART WILL BE ALSO.

MATTHEW 6:20–21 NRSV

There is enough in the world for everyone's need, but not enough for everyone's greed.

FRANK BUCHMAN

41

Going His Way

All our steps are ordered by the Lord.

~ *Proverbs* 20:24 NRSV

A big smile came over Karen's face as she walked down the aisle and accepted her diploma. She had been waiting years for this moment. Now she was sure that at last she was on her way to where God wanted her to go and what he was calling her to do.

From a young age, Karen seemed to move from one interest to another. Even so, she firmly believed God had a plan for her life and that he would reveal it to her when the time was right. "Show me your will," she would pray each day. "Give me the strength to pursue your will with all my heart."

Since that first prayer for guidance, the desire to become a teacher had begun to grow in Karen, and she could now see how perfect a fit it was for her. "Thank you, God," she prayed, "for revealing your will to me and giving me the motivation to stick with it."

Following God's way can sometimes seem uncomfortable. You might wonder where you will end up or what kinds of bumps lay in the road ahead, and sometimes it's a challenge to make sense of what God is calling you to do, especially in the beginning. However, when you follow God's Word and trust in the Lord, you find that he has a perfect plan for you.

Try this: Read in Exodus 40:1–16 about how Moses carefully obeyed God's instructions in the smallest detail. In verse 16, God told Moses how to build the tabernacle, and Moses delegated jobs in order to do it. God allows people to participate with him in carrying out his will. In what areas do you struggle to do God's will?

REMEMBER THE LORD IN EVERYTHING YOU DO, AND HE WILL SHOW YOU THE RIGHT WAY.

PROVERBS 3:6 GNT

SHOW ME THY WAYS, O LORD; TEACH ME THY PATHS.

PSALM 25:4 KJV

To be subjected to God's will is not only to give Him priority in our lives, it is to give Him complete control.

AVERY D. MILLER

CONFIDENCE

The Lord said, "Peter, come over to me."

So Peter began to walk on the sea,

But when his confidence started to shrink

Peter began to falter and sink.

So have confidence in God when storms arise

And rest assured that you'll survive.

Mark Edwards

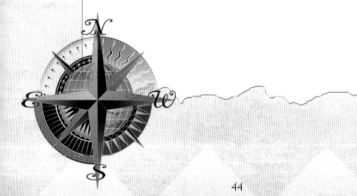

The righteous are as bold as a lion

~ *Proverbs* 28:1 NIV

Do not throw away your confidence, which has a great reward.

~ *Hebrews* 10:35 NASB

WHOEVER DOES NOT RESPECT CONFIDENCE WILL NEVER FIND HAPPINESS IN THEIR PATH.

AUTHOR UNKNOWN

Guarding Your Heart

The human spirit is the lamp of the LORD, searching every innermost part.

~ *Proverbs 20:27* NRSV

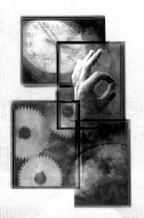

The rules seemed well defined when John was in school. There was no question that cheating on a test or plagiarizing someone's writing was acknowledged as wrong. But when John got a new job after graduation, he found life after school filled with conflicting messages about what was right and what was wrong.

Although John's company stressed high standards, John's boss often cut corners, skipping required procedures to save money and get a jump on the timetable. John didn't want to report his boss's actions, but over time his conscience began to bother him. John decided he would ask God to show him the right course to take. God's answer was simple: listen to your conscience.

John told his boss he would have to speak up about the dangerous short cuts. He would have to speak up, even if it cost him his job. John noticed that after their conversation, his boss was careful to follow procedures whenever they worked together.

🌿 Your conscience is a gift from God that acts as a lamp to help you discern right from wrong in gray and hazy situations. It is the small inner voice that makes you feel conflicted when you are tempted to do something wrong; it's that nagging sense of guilt that follows you afterward until you confess it to God. While you may not like what your conscience tells you, it is always in your best interest to listen to what it's telling you.

🌿 **Try this:** *Write out a plan of action for handling problematic situations. For instance, think of a possible, realistic situation you might encounter and decide your options in advance—I'll walk away, I'll report it, or I'll speak up for what is right—in order to stay true to your conscience.*

ABOVE ALL ELSE, GUARD YOUR HEART, FOR IT IS THE WELLSPRING OF LIFE.

PROVERBS 4:23 NIV

KEEP YOUR CONSCIENCE CLEAR, SO THAT WHEN YOU ARE INSULTED, THOSE WHO SPEAK EVIL OF YOUR GOOD CONDUCT AS FOLLOWERS OF CHRIST WILL BECOME ASHAMED OF WHAT THEY SAY.

1 PETER 3:16 GNT

After God, let us have our conscience as our mentor so that we may know which way the wind is blowing and set our sails accordingly.

SAINT JOHN OF THE LADDER

Staying on the Path

The righteous walk in integrity.

~ *Proverbs 20:7 NRSV*

THE SOULS OF
THE RIGHTEOUS
ARE IN THE HAND
OF GOD.

THE WISDOM OF
SOLOMON 3:1
NRSV

As a graduate, you are equipped with knowledge in your chosen career, and you have acquired the skills necessary to help you succeed. It would be foolish to ignore what you have learned and just wing it. How many people just try to wing it when it comes to their life choices? Why would you want to do that? What would be your chance for success?

Building a righteous life can be understood in the same way. You must apply the biblical concepts you've learned to how you live your life. You must look at the path God has placed before you and stay focused on doing what he asks of you and trusting him to lead you.

Just as you apply the concepts you learned in school to your job, apply what you've learned in God's Word to your life. Righteousness requires a daily commitment on your part to do what is right in the sight of the Lord.

✺ Living a righteous life means living a life that is pleasing to God and consistent with his commandments. Even if you wander from the path, God in his awesome grace will help you get back on track. What's more, the Bible says that when you resist the temptation to conform to the pattern of this world, he will renew your mind. Soon many of the things that presented a temptation for you in the past will lose their power and fade away.

✺ TRY THIS: *Look up the word righteous in the dictionary and see what it means. Then think about some of the people you have met who fit the dictionary definition of a person who lives a righteous life. List some of the characteristics you see in their lives that you think are pleasing to God.*

THE RIGHTEOUSNESS OF THE PERFECT SHALL DIRECT HIS WAY: BUT THE WICKED SHALL FALL BY HIS OWN WICKEDNESS.

PROVERBS 11:5 KJV

STRIVE FOR RIGHTEOUSNESS, GODLINESS, FAITH, LOVE, ENDURANCE, AND GENTLENESS.

I TIMOTHY 6:11 GNT

Truth and kindness in sweet embrace, righteousness and peace are God's grace; for truth out of the earth does spring, and righteousness from heaven ring.

FAYE T. BRESLER

In Its Place

From the fruit of his lips a man is filled with good things as surely as the work of his hands rewards him.

~ *Proverbs 12:14 NIV*

When wealth is lost, nothing is lost; when health is lost, something is lost; when character is lost, all is lost.

Billy Graham

Each day for Darlene was a financial struggle. She waited tables, walked dogs, baby-sat, and cleaned aquariums to make enough money to pay her tuition and monthly bills. She dreamed of the day when she could graduate and get a good job. Shortly after she finished school, she found a job that paid more money than she had ever made before. She was relieved and overjoyed.

Darlene enjoyed the security that her newfound wealth provided, but something was missing. She missed the close connection she had established with God during her college years when she depended upon God to make ends meet. Life then had been financially tenuous, but God had always pulled her through.

As Darlene was praying one day, God revealed to her how unwise it was to put her faith in anyone or anything other than her Savior. She realized that she still needed God to be the foundation in her life, regardless of what her current financial status might be.

Money is an important issue and can influence your spiritual condition. If you lack money, you can worry that God will not provide for you. If you have an abundance of money, you can shift your dependence away from God. Rather than worry about how little or how much money you have, focus on God's promise to provide what you need. Your financial status may change a number of times in your life, but God's steady hand on your life is constant.

Try this: *Consider giving a tenth of your income to God, or you may decide to start with a smaller percentage (such as two percent). As God blesses you, increase your giving. After you begin giving consistently, keep a record of the ways in which God meets your needs and how he does so.*

Get all you can, save all you can, and give all you can.
JOHN WESLEY

No More Worries

Anxiety weighs down the human heart, but a good word cheers it up.

~ *Proverbs 12:25* NRSV

Anxiety does not empty tomorrow of its sorrow, but only empties today of its strength.

Charles Haddon Spurgeon

Oz had been attending school in the U.S. on a student visa and was an excellent student. Graduation was approaching, however, and he knew that he would soon have to return home. He had lost many hours of sleep as a result, and he found it difficult to concentrate. He was anxious about returning to a chaotic home situation.

Oz decided to bring up the matter with a Christian friend at church. "You know, Oz," his friend said, "you have a choice in how you deal with your worries. You can either focus on the difficulties your family is having, or you can believe that God is leading you back for a purpose and will bless you for following his will."

Oz asked God to help him see the Lord's vision of the future rather than his own limited perspective. As Oz gave control to God and meditated on his promises, he began to feel his worries ease and slip away.

x

Anxiety is a normal part of life and can help to stimulate creative thinking and problem solving. But constant anxiety can cloud your judgment and rob you of the joy God wants you to have, and it could be detrimental to your health. Make a constant decision to look past the difficulties in your situation and free your mind of worry and anxiety. As you release yourself into God's care, he will fill you with his peace.

Try this: When you feel anxious, take a moment to isolate what is causing the stress. Schedule time to share your worries with a close friend or family member or pastor at your church and then ask that person to pray with you about the situation until you are able to release it to God.

THE LORD WILL BE YOUR CONFIDENCE AND WILL KEEP YOUR FOOT FROM BEING CAUGHT.

PROVERBS 3:26 NASB

DO NOT BE ANXIOUS ABOUT ANYTHING, BUT IN EVERYTHING, BY PRAYER AND PETITION, WITH THANKSGIVING, PRESENT YOUR REQUESTS TO GOD.

PHILIPPIANS 4:6 NIV

Every tomorrow has two handles. We can take hold of it by the handle of anxiety or by the handle of faith.

AUTHOR UNKNOWN

Contentment

Humble let me live and die,

Nor long for Midas' golden touch;

If Heaven more generous gifts deny,

I shall not miss them much,—

Too grateful for the blessing lent

Of simple tastes and mind content.

Oliver Wendell Holmes

*Don't make me either
poor or rich, but give me
only the bread
I need each day.*

~ *Proverbs* 30:8 NIrV

*I have learned this secret,
so that anywhere, at any
time, I am content. . . . I
have the strength to face all
conditions by the power that
Christ gives me.*

~ *Philippians* 4:12–13 GNT

THE BEST AND
MOST BEAUTIFUL
THINGS IN THIS
WORLD CANNOT BE
SEEN OR EVEN
HEARD, BUT MUST
BE FELT WITH
THE HEART.

HELEN KELLER

God Gives Good Things

The blessing of the LORD makes rich, and he adds no sorrow with it.

~ *Proverbs 10:22* NRSV

PRAISE GOD,
FROM WHOM
ALL BLESSINGS
FLOW! PRAISE
HIM, ALL
CREATURES
HERE BELOW!

THOMAS KEN

When Jill decided to move to a new town after graduation, she missed all her old friends. She knew she would have to make new ones, but she really didn't know how. She had grown up with all her friends, and she'd never had to go out of her way to make new ones. This was the first time she'd ever had to seek out relationships.

As Jill was out walking one day, she noticed a church a short distance from her house. She decided to attend on Sunday, and there she met a wonderful group of young people. When they found out she was new in town, they went out of their way to include her in their activities and to ask her to join them even outside of church.

Having this new group of friends was a wonderful blessing for Jill. "Thank you, Lord," she whispered, "for all your blessings."

Did a friend give you a compliment today that made you feel good about yourself? Did a new opportunity for personal growth cross your path? Did something else happen that made your day a bit brighter? Little blessings happen every day, and they are reminders of the great blessings of God's love and tender care. Take the time to focus on God's blessings both great and small, and give him thanks and praise for the all the blessings he places in your life.

Try this: As a way of thanking God for the blessings he has placed in your life, think about some person you can bless. That might be helping someone with a chore, offering an encouraging word, or giving money to help with a financial need. Now keep going. Find another person to bless.

EVERY GOOD AND PERFECT GIFT IS FROM ABOVE, COMING DOWN FROM THE FATHER OF THE HEAVENLY LIGHTS, WHO DOES NOT CHANGE LIKE SHIFTING SHADOWS.

JAMES 1:17 NIV

BLESSED BE THE GOD AND FATHER OF OUR LORD JESUS CHRIST, WHO HAS BLESSED US WITH EVERY SPIRITUAL BLESSING IN THE HEAVENLY PLACES IN CHRIST.

EPHESIANS 1:3 NASB

MYSELF IN CONSTANT GOOD HEALTH, AND IN A MOST HANDSOME AND THRIVING CONDITION, BLESSED BE ALMIGHTY GOD FOR IT.

SAMUEL PEPYS

It's Time to Step Out

An honest person is as brave as a lion.

~ Proverbs 28:1 GNT

Peter and John prayed together to the Lord, "Enable your servants to speak your word with great boldness."

Acts 4:29 NIV

Since he was a young boy, Brad had been following the careful path that his parents had laid out. Now, as graduation from high school approached, he found himself under mounting pressure to go immediately off to college. Brad, however, felt God was telling him to take his time to determine what he wanted to do in life. He didn't know quite yet what that would involve, but he desired to follow God's leading.

After wrestling for several days with what to tell his parents, he prayed. "God, please give me boldness to talk with Mom and Dad, and give me the confidence that I'm doing the right thing." When Brad finished praying, he felt spiritually and emotionally stronger.

Brad thanked God for giving him the courage to talk with his mother and father. And when he lovingly and respectfully presented his point of view, his parents supported his decision.

In *The Wizard of Oz*, one trip to see the Wizard was all the Cowardly Lion needed to be filled with courage. In real life, receiving boldness is a more gradual process. As you approach various situations in your life, God will help you handle each circumstance. Seeing God help you meet each challenge in an appropriate manner will make you bolder and more confident in yourself, but even more confident in God.

Try this: *Do something specific that you normally would be too timid to try. Strike up a conversation with a new person at church, invite an acquaintance to dinner, or share with another individual something personal that God did for you this week. Be aware of how each of these small successes can strengthen you spiritually and emotionally.*

On the day I called, you answered me; you made me bold with strength in my soul.

Psalm 138:3 NASB

Let us therefore come boldly unto the throne of grace, that we may obtain mercy, and find grace to help in time of need.

Hebrews 4:16 KJV

Stand upright, speak thy thoughts, declare the truth thou hast that all may share; be bold, proclaim it everywhere: They only live who dare.

Lewis Morris

Room to Grow

Love covers over all wrongs.

~ *Proverbs 10:12* NIV

Gloria and Becky became best friends in college. They shared their dreams, ambitions, and passing fancies with each other.

After graduation, Gloria went back to Chicago, and Becky moved to Boston to start a new job. Gloria wrote letters, sent e-mail messages, and called Becky once a week. Becky did the same for the first few months, but then she contacted Gloria less and less frequently. Eventually she stopped altogether.

For a while, Gloria felt hurt and disappointed. Becky seemed to be making new friends and settling into a new life without her. Gloria prayed about it, and then she remembered: *Love frees rather than binds*. "Lord," she prayed, "help me to show Becky my love by setting aside my hurt and disappointment."

Gloria continued to keep touch with Becky. Before long, the two had once again created a bond, even stronger and more cherished. This time the bond allowed both the freedom to grow.

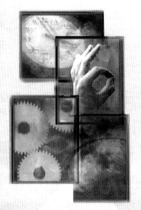

The type of love modeled in the New Testament is a selfless love that puts the welfare of the other person first. That love releases, forgives, and puts aside bitterness, resentment, hurt, and disappointment. God exhibited that love for you when he sent Jesus to give his life for you. Consider how much you really love the people in your life, and ask yourself if you are willing to put their feelings, welfare, and personal growth before your own.

TRY THIS: *If there is a friend or loved one in your life who has hurt or disappointed you, renew your commitment of love to that person by choosing to overlook the offense. Ask yourself if you are holding on too tight or if you are expecting too much from that person. Ask God to give you clear perspective.*

LOVE ONE ANOTHER DEEPLY, FROM THE HEART.

I PETER 1:22 NIV

ALL OF YOU, HAVE UNITY OF SPIRIT, SYMPATHY, LOVE FOR ONE ANOTHER. A TENDER HEART, AND A HUMBLE MIND.

I PETER 3:8 NRSV

TO LOVE IS TO WILL THE GOOD OF ANOTHER.

SAINT THOMAS AQUINAS

Seeking God's Favor

Anyone who looks for what is good finds favor.

— Proverbs 11:27 NIrV

Tyler admired his dad and wanted him to be proud of him. That was a big reason why Tyler drove himself to succeed.

Tyler moved away from home after graduation to begin life on his own, but still he sought his father's favor in everything he did. As he was praying one day, he realized that he should be seeking his heavenly Father's favor as well. .

"How do I please you, Lord?" he asked. "How do I know to do your will?" As he continued to pray, Tyler understood. It was the same way he received his earthly father's favor—by seeking him out, listening to his counsel, and honoring him with his actions. He would pray, read his Bible, and listen for God's voice. Tyler decided right then that his life would be well spent seeking to please both his wonderful fathers—his heavenly Father as well as his earthly father.

It is marvelous to discover that God doesn't favor one person over another. The Bible says he pours out his favor on all those who wholeheartedly seek to do his will and live a righteous life. It makes no difference who you are or how long you have known him. Whenever you approach God, he will say, "Come to me. You are welcome. I'm happy to see you. You are my favored child."

TRY THIS: *Look up the word favor in a dictionary or thesaurus and make a list of all its synonyms: kindness, esteem, liking, goodwill, approval. These are just a few. Make the list as long as you can. Then pray for favor, reading into your prayer all the words on the list.*

A GOOD MAN OBTAINS FAVOR FROM THE LORD.

PROVERBS 12:2 NIV

FOR SURELY, O LORD, YOU BLESS THE RIGHTEOUS; YOU SURROUND THEM WITH YOUR FAVOR AS WITH A SHIELD.

PSALM 5:12 NIV

When God and his glory are made our end, we shall find a silent likeness pass in upon us; the beauty of God will, by degrees, enter upon our soul.

STEPHEN CHARNOCK

CHARACTER

Forget the slander you have heard;
Forget the hasty, unkind word.
Forget the chap whose sour face
Forgets to smile in any place.
Forget you're not a millionaire;
Forget the mess that is your hair.
Forget the coffee when it's cold;
Forget to kick, forget to scold.
Forget the quarrel and the cause;
Forget the whole affair, because
When you forget all that is wrong
It shows the world
your character is strong.

Author Unknown

*Whoever is steadfast
in righteousness will live.*

~ *Proverbs* 11:19 NRSV

*You will keep in perfect
peace him whose mind
is steadfast, because he
trusts in you, LORD.*

~ *Isaiah* 26:3 NIV

CHARACTER IS
MUCH EASIER KEPT
THAN RECOVERED.

THOMAS PAINE

Afraid of Nothing

The fear of others lays a snare, but one who trusts in the LORD is secure.

~ Proverbs 29:25 NRSV

LET ME ASSERT
MY FIRM BELIEF
THAT THE ONLY
THING WE HAVE
TO FEAR IS FEAR
ITSELF.

FRANKLIN D.
ROOSEVELT

Shannon was glad to be done with school, but the thought of leaving home after graduation and living on her own made her fearful. This would be the first time she would be living totally alone—no family, no roommate. She worried. Will I be safe living all by myself?

Shannon's persistent fears soon turned what should have been a challenging situation into a terrifying dilemma. She quaked at every sound, and she kept the light on even while she slept. However, one day as she pondered her predicament, she noticed a sparrow outside her window and thought of the words in the praise song, "His eye is on the sparrow, and I know He watches me."

Shannon realized how foolish it was to live in fear, for God was always with her to care for her. Bowing her head, she recommitted herself to God. As she did, her fears began to lift and take flight, just like the wings of the little sparrow.

꧁ Fear is God-given. When you are confronted with a dangerous situation, fear heightens your senses and urges you to get up and out of the way before you get hurt. It is designed to keep you alive and well. Fear should be part of your experience, but it need not dominate your life. The Bible says that God has not given you a spirit of fear, but a spirit of power, and love, and a sound mind.

꧁ TRY THIS: *Choose one area where fear has the upper hand—heights, confrontation, darkness. Using a topical Bible concordance, find scriptures that encourage you to stand up to your fear. Read these verses every day. Then, when a challenge comes, call these verses to mind, remember what you've learned, and stand firm.*

WHOEVER LISTENS TO [WISDOM] WILL HAVE SECURITY. HE WILL BE SAFE, WITH NO REASON TO BE AFRAID.

PROVERBS 1:33 GNT

YOU DID NOT RECEIVE A SPIRIT THAT MAKES YOU A SLAVE AGAIN TO FEAR, BUT YOU RECEIVED THE SPIRIT OF SONSHIP. AND BY HIM WE CRY, "ABBA, FATHER."

ROMANS 8:15 NIV

Fear the Lord and you will do everything well.

SHEPHERD OF HERMAS

The Real World

Preserve sound judgment and discernment, do not let them out of your sight.

~ *Proverbs 3:21 NIV*

Common sense is the knack of seeing things as they are, and doing things as they ought to be done.

Josh Billings

"Not that way, Peter. We need to turn it so that its weight becomes a fulcrum." John was helping Peter move into his new apartment. Peter had learned how to work with others, follow directions, and work hard. He could master difficult material and measure up to any test given.

"You're right, John. You're sure a master when it comes to common sense," Peter said. Peter knew he needed to work on the ability to think through a situation, weigh the consequences of each possible action, and then exercise good judgment before proceeding. As Peter thought about this, he asked God to use John to guide Peter and help him learn to make wise decisions. "Say, how about letting me bounce a few ideas off you from time to time?"

Peter prayed that he would learn from listening to John and would grow wiser and stronger from his mistakes.

⁘ God wants you to make good decisions that will spare you unnecessary hardship. He will use many means to guide you: your quiet time with him, the advice of another trusted individual in your life, or a passage in Scripture, as well as your bad choices, mistakes, and accidents. Turn to him first when you face an unfamiliar situation and be open to different ways that he may lead you. Each time you make a wise choice or handle a situation appropriately, you will gain elements of good sense.

⁘ TRY THIS: *Seek the advice of two or three people regarding something in your life that requires good sense—seeking a new job, deciding whether to buy a new or used car, evaluating safe and affordable places to live, and other such major decisions. Pray over each suggestion that these persons give you and ask God to reveal to you what is the best course of action.*

FOLLY IS JOY TO HIM WHO LACKS SENSE, BUT A MAN OF UNDERSTANDING WALKS STRAIGHT.

PROVERBS 15:21
NASB

THE KING SAID TO DANIEL, "I HAVE HEARD THAT THE SPIRIT OF THE HOLY GODS IS IN YOU AND THAT YOU ARE SKILLFUL AND HAVE KNOWLEDGE AND WISDOM."

DANIEL 5:14 GNT

Common sense is the measure of the possible; it is composed of experience and prevision; it is calculation applied to life.

HENRI-FREDERIC AMIEL

Pointing the Way

Those who lead others to do what is right are wise.

~ Proverbs 11:30 NIrV

BLESSED IS THE
LEADER WHO
SEEKS THE BEST
FOR THOSE HE
SERVES.

AUTHOR
UNKNOWN

In school, Robert had always been content to sit back and let others take the lead roles in class discussions and group projects. He had good ideas, but he didn't have the desire to stand out in a crowd or to persuade others to follow his course of action. When he accepted a job after graduation, he fully expected to remain a team player at his new company.

His new coworkers, however, soon sensed Robert's insightfulness and creativity, and he realized that God was revealing a future role for him. God had given Robert a talent for leading and inspiring others.

Robert watched other successful leaders in the company, and he worked hard to learn from them and to emulate them. He was excited and challenged by this new role that God had revealed to him, and he learned to depend more and more on God's wisdom and support.

Even if you consider yourself a follower rather than a leader, you could be called on at some point to actively lead another person through some struggle. Although it is true that God bestows certain people with extraordinary leadership gifts, you too can serve as a leader when God sets a challenge before you. Trust him to guide you, and freely accept the responsibility when it comes your way.

Try this: Think about the qualities you have seen in people who are good leaders. What skills do those individuals have that make others want to follow them? Choose two specific people — a boss, a pastor, a political leader, a teacher — and compile a list of admirable qualities you see in them. Decide which of these qualities you'd like to emulate in your own life.

THOSE WHO PLAN WHAT IS GOOD FIND LOVE AND FAITHFULNESS.

PROVERBS 14:22 NIV

REMEMBER YOUR FORMER LEADERS, WHO SPOKE GOD'S MESSAGE TO YOU. THINK BACK ON HOW THEY LIVED AND DIED, AND IMITATE THEIR FAITH.

HEBREWS 13:7 GNT

Christian leadership . . . appears to break down into five main ingredients — clear vision, hard work, dogged perseverance, humble service and iron discipline.

JOHN R. W. STOTT

71

Speaking the Truth

A faithful witness does not lie.

~ *Proverbs* 14:5 NRSV

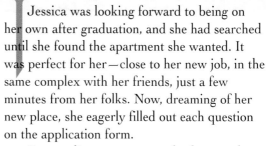

Jessica was looking forward to being on her own after graduation, and she had searched until she found the apartment she wanted. It was perfect for her—close to her new job, in the same complex with her friends, just a few minutes from her folks. Now, dreaming of her new place, she eagerly filled out each question on the application form.

But a policy statement on the form made her hesitate. The pet deposit was $500, and Jessica had a pet cat that she adored. Knowing that she didn't have the money, Jessica wavered, then scribbled down zero for the number of pets she owned.

Jessica got the apartment. But guilt made her shy away from making new friends in the complex, and she could barely face her landlord. Finally, she realized God was telling her to come clean and admit the truth to her landlord. It wasn't easy coming up with the money, but after confessing, Jessica felt a burden lift from her shoulders.

God wants you to be honest in all your words and deeds. He knows that deceit and mistrust can cause damage to your inner sense of integrity, your relationship with God, and your relationships with others. Carrying around guilt and deception is likely to inhibit and exhaust you, but having nothing to hide is a great blessing. The saying really is true, "What a tangled web we weave, when first we practice to deceive."

Try this: List some of the times that you have answered others dishonestly because you believed the truth would hurt them. Write down some of the ways you rationalized dishonesty (such as "it's just a little white lie" or "it's for his or her own good."). Think about ways that you can be both truthful and kind when similar situations arise in the future.

Truthful lips will be established forever, but a lying tongue is only for a moment.

PROVERBS 12:19
NASB

WE pray to God that you will do no wrong—not in order to show that we are a success, but so that you may do what is right, even though we may seem to be failures.

2 CORINTHIANS 13:7
GNT

It does not require many words to speak the truth.

CHIEF JOSEPH

Wisdom

Wisdom is more valuable than jewels;
nothing you could want can compare with it.
Wisdom offers you long life,
as well as wealth and honor.
Wisdom can make your life pleasant
and lead you safely through it.
Those who become wise are happy;
wisdom will give them life.
The Lord created the earth by his wisdom;
by his knowledge he set the sky in place.
His wisdom caused the rivers to flow
and the clouds to give rain to the earth.

Proverbs 3:15–20 GNT

If you are wise, your wisdom will reward you.

~ *Proverbs 9:12 NIrV*

If any of you lacks wisdom, he should ask God, who gives generously to all without finding fault, and it will be given to him.

~ *James 1:5 NIV*

WISDOM IS, AND STARTS WITH, THE HUMILITY TO ACCEPT THE FACT THAT YOU DON'T HAVE ALL THE RIGHT ANSWERS, AND THE COURAGE TO LEARN TO ASK THE RIGHT QUESTIONS.

AUTHOR UNKNOWN

Sowing and Reaping

A generous man will prosper; he who refreshes others will himself be refreshed.

~ *Proverbs 11:25 NIV*

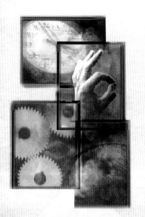

Generosity is always putting other peoples' wants and needs before your own.

Author Unknown

Joe believed in doing his part for the church and giving ten percent of his income as a tithe, but this sometimes placed an overwhelming financial burden on him as a student. When he got a good job after graduation, he looked forward to having a little extra income so that tithing wasn't such a strain.

After a few weeks of fulfilling the exactness of his tithe, however, Joe came to understand that God wanted more. Joe needed to do more than just rest secure in his own means and do only "his part." God wanted him to go a step further. God was encouraging Joe to give more than the standard ten percent each week as a sign of Joe's commitment.

Joe was tentative with this at first, but he soon discovered that giving freely from his heart brought him incredible joy. And the guidance God offered was based in sound judgment as well as increased generosity.

Many people find it easier to give to others than to accept what others give to them. Just as God wants you to be generous, he wants you to allow his generosity to flow to you and be a blessing to you. Open your heart to both give and receive from others as the need arises.

Try this: *Take a moment to reflect on something generous that someone has recently done for you. Write that person a thank-you note that expresses your gratitude and lets that individual know what his or her generosity meant to you. Be sure also to speak a word of thanks to God.*

A GENEROUS MAN WILL HIMSELF BE BLESSED, FOR HE SHARES HIS FOOD WITH THE POOR.

PROVERBS 22:9 NIV

BE RICH IN GOOD WORDS, TO BE GENEROUS AND READY TO SHARE WITH OTHERS.

I TIMOTHY 6:18 GNT

Do all the good you can, by all the means you can, in all the ways you can, in all the places you can, at all the times you can, to all the people you can, as long as ever you can.

JOHN WESLEY

For Your Own Good

When the Lord corrects you, pay close attention.

~ *Proverbs 3:11 GNT*

LOVE IS AT THE
ROOT OF ALL
HEALTHY
DISCIPLINE.

FRED ROGERS

Jennifer's boss had just corrected her, and it rankled her a little bit. It reminded Jennifer of being back in school. Her instructor would pose a question, and she would raise her hand, thinking she knew the answer. She would begin to give an explanation, only to have the instructor cut her off by saying, "Well, that's not quite what I was looking for."

Jennifer's first response was to feel embarrassed and stifled. In school it had taken her two full semesters before she learned to step past her initial reaction and listen to the teacher's words of wisdom and experience.

Jennifer had to give herself a bit of a pep talk. She knew that this job, her first, was simply another level of learning. To get the most out of it, she would have to carry her productive attitude toward correction into the workplace. "Lord, please help me to receive this correction with grace."

A ship that veers off course even one degree on one side of the Atlantic is doomed to be hundreds of miles off course by the time it reaches the other side. The captain of the vessel must make any correction quickly or lose precious time and compensation. The same is true in life. A little correction could make the critical difference between success and failure. It means putting your ego on hold, but it pays big rewards as your voyage progresses.

Try this: Think about someone in your life who truly cares for you and has your best interests at heart, someone who can also be honest about your shortcomings. Ask that person to be your accountability partner—someone with whom you you can go to check out whether you've handled a difficult situation correctly, someone who will then pray about it with you.

He who heeds discipline shows the way to life, but whoever ignores correction leads others astray.

Proverbs 10:17 NIV

The Lord corrects those he loves, as parents correct a child of whom they are proud.

Proverbs 3:12 GNT

Discipline is the secret of godliness. You must learn to discipline yourself for the purpose of godliness.

Jay Adams

The Wisdom of Others

Plans are established by taking advice.

~ *Proverbs 20:18* NRSV

Erica knew that she could always turn to her pastor at church for advice when she had a difficult problem. She had only been in the sixth grade when she had first gone to him for help. He always seemed to know exactly what to say and do, and Erica depended upon his wisdom. Now, as she prepared to move away for college, she wondered how she could replace that stabilizing factor in her life.

When she raised this question with the pastor, he said, "You know, Erica, I've just passed on to you the wisdom I have gained from my relationship with God, my study of the Bible, and my experience. I'm not the source of that wisdom—God is. Ask him to advise you, and he will send wise people into your life."

That evening, Erica thanked God for the wisdom she had received from her pastor, and thanked him for the counselors he would send to her in the future.

꿍 How do you know if any suggestion you're given is good or bad advice? Check to see if it corresponds with the teachings in the Bible, and then take it to God in prayer and ask him to help you see clearly if the advice is credible. Talk it over also with a trusted person. Even the book of Proverbs acknowledges that there is safety in an abundance of counselors.

꿍 TRY THIS: *The next time someone gives you advice (you probably won't have to wait long) listen carefully and write it down. Open your mind to truly consider the point of view of the advice giver. Then check to see what the Bible says on the subject. And pray that God will move you to the correct decision.*

WHERE THERE IS NO GUIDANCE, A NATION FALLS, BUT IN AN ABUNDANCE OF COUNSELORS THERE IS SAFETY.

PROVERBS 11:14 NRSV

THE HEART OF THE DISCERNING ACQUIRES KNOWLEDGE; THE EARS OF THE WISE SEEK IT OUT.

PROVERBS 18:15 NIV

Write down the advice of him who loves you, though you like it not at present.

AUTHOR UNKNOWN

My Word Is My Bond

A good name is to be chosen rather than great riches.

~ *Proverbs 22:1 NRSV*

A GOOD NAME,
LIKE GOOD WILL,
IS GOT BY MANY
ACTIONS AND
LOST BY ONE.

LORD JEFFERY

Phil didn't think of himself as having any particular reputation at school. He wasn't a member of the in-crowd or a member of any fraternity. Nor did he desire to be. He was happy simply going to class each day, studying hard, and having quiet friendships. He tried to live a life according to the principles he found in the Bible. In his mind, he was just a regular guy.

But these qualities made Phil stand out, and his reputation began to grow around the campus. He gained the respect of anyone who talked with him. After graduation, one of his instructors passed his name along to an employer as a good candidate who would be dependable, hard-working, and honest.

Phil was thrilled when he was offered his dream job. "Thank you, God," he prayed, "for helping me develop a reputation that reflects positively on you. Help me to keep my reputation strong as I enter this new phase of my life."

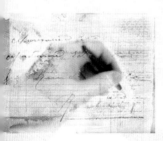

A good reputation is as productive as it is wonderful. It will give you favor with people when you need it most and bring many worthwhile opportunities your way. Building and maintaining a good reputation takes time and effort. A good reputation is an invaluable investment in your future, and yet it is one you can afford, regardless of what your economic status might be.

Try this: *Think about what having a good reputation means to you, and what qualities a person must have to obtain one. Read a short biography on a reputable person like Mother Teresa or Billy Graham and consider their qualities alongside yours. Consider which desirable qualities you might want to cultivate in your own life.*

It is a maxim with me that no man was ever written out of reputation but by himself.

RICHARD BENTLEY

Integrity

True worth is in being, not seeming—

In doing, each day that goes by,

Some little good—not in dreaming

Of great things to do by and by.

For whatever men say in their blindness,

And in spite of the fancies of youth,

There's nothing so kingly as kindness,

And nothing so royal as truth.

Alice Cary

*Whoever walks in
integrity walks securely.*
— *Proverbs* 10:9 NRSV

*The integrity of the
upright guides them.*
— *Proverbs* 11:3 NIV

REAL INTEGRITY
STAYS IN PLACE
WHETHER THE TEST
IS ADVERSITY OR
PROSPERITY.

CHARLES SWINDOLL

Being True

The faithful will abound with blessings.

~ *Proverbs 28:20* NRSV

Tracy was convinced that God was calling her to pursue a career in journalism. She loved interviewing people and looking at each angle of an issue to piece together a complete story. In school, she had faithfully pursued her goal, and now that she had graduated, she looked forward to a career as a reporter on one of the major newspapers.

But after a month of looking, Tracy had no success finding a job in her field. Well-intentioned friends and family started questioning whether she had chosen the right profession. They urged her to consider trying to find a job in another area. She almost wavered, and she even went so far as to interview for several positions outside of journalism.

Finally though, Tracy decided to stand firm, letting nothing distract her from what God had called her to do. "Lord," she prayed, "please give me the strength to remain steadfast to you." God rewarded Tracy's faithfulness, and the right opportunity soon came her way.

Constancy is an important quality. Loyalty to a goal can provide the motivation to keep reaching for more of life. Steadfastness in relationships can provide the support needed to keep pursuing dreams. Faithfulness to God can ensure that you will have the resources you need to succeed. When you're tempted to quit, spend some time thinking about how faithful God has been to you. He never quits.

THE LORD GUARDS THE COURSE OF THE JUST AND PROTECTS THE WAY OF HIS FAITHFUL.

PROVERBS 2:8 NIV

TRY THIS: Take a few steps to build greater constancy in your life. Make one new commitment—diet, exercise, church attendance. Write down what you are committing to do and for how long before you begin. Keep a record for four weeks and then evaluate your progress. Do you see evidence of more constancy in your life?

JESUS SAID, "WHOEVER CAN BE TRUSTED WITH VERY LITTLE CAN ALSO BE TRUSTED WITH MUCH."

LUKE 16:10 NIV

Faithless is he that says farewell when the road darkens.

J. R. R. TOLKIEN

The Closest Circle

Teach children how they should live, and they will remember it all their life.

~ Proverbs 22:6 GNT

IT IS IN THE LOVE OF ONE'S FAMILY ONLY THAT HEARTFELT HAPPINESS IS KNOWN.

THOMAS JEFFERSON

Amber looked forward to the wonderful changes and opportunities that graduation would bring to her, although her excitement was bittersweet. In order to take advantage of those opportunities, she was going to have to leave her family behind as she pursued her new career.

When she moved to another city to take a job, she found herself lonely. She longed for the comfort of home. She talked to her parents and siblings on the phone at least twice a week, and she drove the several hours home every few months.

Amber was happy that her relationship with her family members remained strong despite the distance between them. Her connection with them had to do with the love in their hearts for each other rather than on their constant proximity.

Even when she met a wonderful young man and married, even when she and her husband had children and established their own family unit, her love for the people back home never wavered.

The Bible says that there isn't anything in this world that can separate you from God's loving presence. This includes trouble and hardship, distance and time, life and death. Just as you keep in touch with your earthly family, you must also keep in touch with your heavenly Father, God. Keeping in touch means finding time to talk no matter how busy your life may be.

Try this: *Take time during the next few weeks to remember your family and all the love, caring, and generosity they have shown to you. Show your appreciation by sending members of your family a card or short note telling them how much they mean to you. Make a commitment not to let more than a month elapse between phone calls to your parents.*

Listen to your father; without him you would not exist. When your mother is old, show her your appreciation.

PROVERBS 23:22
GNT

Jesus said, "Whoever does the will of My Father who is in heaven, he is My brother and sister and mother."

MATTHEW 12:50
NASB

The most powerful lessons about ethics and morality . . . come from family life where people treat one another with respect, consideration, and love.

NEIL KURSHAN

What Drives You?

All deeds are right in the sight of the doer, but the LORD weighs the heart.

~ *Proverbs 21:2 NRSV*

In all our actions, God considers the intention: whether we act for Him or for some other motive.

Saint Maximus the Confessor

From a young age Jim learned from his parents and Sunday school teachers that the way to follow God was to serve at church, and he did so earnestly. When the time came he enrolled in Bible college so that he could one day become a minister.

After graduation, Jim accepted a position as youth pastor at a community church. The people were good to him and he liked them, but after a few months, Jim realized his life lacked joy, and he began to feel like he was only going through the motions. He knew that the young people he was attempting to serve deserved better.

As Jim sought God about his dilemma, he realized that his motive for entering the ministry had been misinformed—the ministry was only one way to serve God. Through prayer and counseling, Jim recognized that perhaps he had been following his own agenda for his life rather than God's.

90

It's possible to do the right things for the wrong motives and the wrong things for the right motives. That's why it is important to examine your motives honestly and often to be sure that you are pursuing goals that are in line with the gifts and abilities God has There will be an accompanying sense of joy and satisfaction in what you're doing when you are doing the right thing for the right motive.

Try this: In the center of a sheet of paper, write down a goal, and draw a circle around it. Note why this goal is appealing to you, such as money, self-satisfaction, or working with others. List the steps necessary to accomplish your goal. Develop a timeline. to accomplish that particular goal and connect your motivations to your goal. Are any adjustments needed?

You may think everything you do is right, but the Lord judges your motives.

Proverbs 16:2 GNT

The Lord searches every heart and understands every motive behind the thoughts.

1 Chronicles 28:9 NIV

Love is the impetus, service the act, and creativity the result.

Sarah Patton Boyle

At Any Price

When pride comes, then comes disgrace, but with humility comes wisdom.
~ *Proverbs* 11:2 NIV

IDLENESS AND PRIDE TAX WITH A HEAVIER HAND THAN KINGS AND GOVERNMENTS.

Benjamin Franklin

Dan's father had instilled in his son the importance of taking pride in everything he did. Dan had learned this lesson well. He made the dean's list in school, and he graduated with honors. His excellent preparation paved the way for him to land a great job.

It was then that Dan exhibited another kind of pride—a selfish pride that caused him to have trouble admitting his mistakes. He found that he couldn't let go of an idea, even if it obviously wasn't working.

At his first job evaluation, Dan's boss told him, "Dan, your work is excellent. But there is no room in this company for a person who can't respect and appreciate the strengths of others. No one is right all the time—even you. Until you understand that, you will find it difficult to succeed." Dan prayed about what his boss had said and asked God to help him conquer the pride that was becoming his stumbling block.

The right kind of pride that causes you to seek satisfaction in doing things well is a productive form that will help you reach your goals and establish your self-respect. Another form of pride, however, is destructive. It causes you to have an overly exalted opinion of yourself. The Bible states that you should avoid thinking of yourself more highly than you ought. Instead, you should think of yourself soberly, understanding the talents God has placed in your life.

Try this: Stop on occasion and give yourself a pride check. Ask yourself whether a particular action or attitude causes you to (1) feel good about yourself or (2) feel better than someone else. The first is a sign of good pride; the second should serve as a warning that trouble is on the way.

PRIDE LEADS TO DESTRUCTION, AND ARROGANCE TO DOWNFALL.

PROVERBS 16:18 GNT

EACH ONE SHOULD TEST HIS OWN ACTIONS. THEN HE CAN TAKE PRIDE IN HIMSELF, WITHOUT COMPARING HIMSELF TO SOMEBODY ELSE.

GALATIANS 6:4 NIV

To be proud and inaccessible is to be timid and weak
JEAN BAPTISTE MASSILLON

SUCCESS

O LORD, GRANT US SUCCESS.
BLESSED IS HE WHO COMES
IN THE NAME OF THE LORD.
FROM THE HOUSE OF THE LORD WE BLESS YOU.
THE LORD IS GOD, AND HE HAS MADE
HIS LIGHT SHINE UPON US.
WITH BOUGHS IN HAND,
JOIN IN THE FESTAL PROCESSION
UP TO THE HORNS OF THE ALTAR.
YOU ARE MY GOD, AND I WILL GIVE YOU THANKS;
YOU ARE MY GOD, AND I WILL EXALT YOU.
GIVE THANKS TO THE LORD, FOR HE IS GOOD;
HIS LOVE ENDURES FOREVER.
PSALM 118:25–29 NIV

Commit to the LORD everything you do. Then your plans will succeed.

~ *Proverbs 16:3 NIrV*

Save us, LORD, save us! Give us success, O LORD!

~ *Psalm 118:25 GNT*

If at first you don't succeed; you are running about average.

M. H. Alderson

Singing from the Heart

Those who do right can expect joy.

~ *Proverbs* 10:28 NRSV

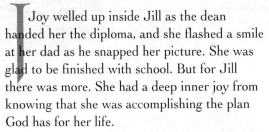

REAL JOY COMES
NOT FROM EASE
OR RICHES OR
FROM THE PRAISE
OF MEN, BUT
FROM DOING
SOMETHING
WORTHWHILE.

PIERRE CORNEILLE

Joy welled up inside Jill as the dean handed her the diploma, and she flashed a smile at her dad as he snapped her picture. She was glad to be finished with school. But for Jill there was more. She had a deep inner joy from knowing that she was accomplishing the plan God has for her life.

Jill thanked the Lord for fulfilling his promises to her and for helping to keep her steadfast through the years of work and preparation. "Thank you, God, for guiding me to the right school, helping me to be accepted, and encouraging me to trust you for my tuition and expenses. You said you would take care of those things if I followed you, and you did."

Jill knew that life after graduation would be filled with challenges even greater than those she'd faced in school. She was ready. She knew the joy she had already found in pursuing God's will would see her through, and she was ready to keep going.

The Bible says that true joy, unlike happiness, is unaffected by your external circumstances. Joy is related to being at peace with God and living a life that's pleasing to him. The Bible urges Christians to rejoice even when they face difficult times. That might seem like an impossible task. It is a joyous task, however, when you know and serve God. His joy flows in and through you as you live your life according to his will and purposes.

TRY THIS: Test your joy quotient by making a list of the top five things that make you happy in life. Move down the list and ask yourself what you would do if that particular item was no longer part of your life. Would you continue to be able to rejoice in God's love and grace?

THERE IS . . . JOY FOR THOSE WHO PROMOTE PEACE.

PROVERBS 12:20 NIV

YOU HAVE MADE KNOWN TO ME THE PATH OF LIFE, O LORD; YOU WILL FILL ME WITH JOY IN YOUR PRESENCE, WITH ETERNAL PLEASURES AT YOUR RIGHT HAND.

PSALM 16:11 NIV

The best way to show our gratitude to God and people is to accept everything with joy.

MOTHER TERESA

Continuing to Grow

Let the wise listen and add to their learning.
~ *Proverbs* 1:5 NIV

When Brian finished his last class on the way to getting his degree in software development, he thought that he would be able to relax a bit. It hadn't sunk in yet that in his field in particular the classes would never really end. Rapid technological advancements ensured that Brian would continually return to school for recertification in the latest software developments.

In a similar way, Brian knew that his life as a Christian was also a lifelong learning process. It seemed that just when he thought he had a particular biblical principle worked out, God would speak to his heart and bring new ideas into his mind. Brian thanked God for putting him in a career that continually challenged his mind, and he also thanked him for a faith that was constantly challenging his soul.

"Lord," he prayed, "help to grow intellectually, but also help me to be more committed to spiritual growth than I am to career growth. Keep me always aware of what's really important."

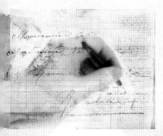

Knowledge is gained primarily through the situations you encounter and the ways in which you handle each particular circumstance. The experiences you have will provide the greatest source of continual learning in your life and shape your perceptions of the world, and so it is important to make God a part of those experiences. God will open your mind and reveal new and incredible things about his nature. And as your knowledge grows, he will gradually shape you according to his will.

TRY THIS: *Schedule a learning enrichment day. Use this day to research several subjects that you would like to tackle after graduation. This might be a cooking class, a computer class, or a seminar on a subject you enjoy. Before the end of the day, settle on one particular thing, find out the particulars, and make plans to attend.*

ANYTHING YOU SAY TO THE WISE WILL MAKE THEM WISER. WHATEVER YOU TELL THE RIGHTEOUS WILL ADD TO THEIR KNOWLEDGE.

PROVERBS 9:9 GNT

GROW IN THE GRACE AND KNOWLEDGE OF OUR LORD AND SAVIOR JESUS CHRIST.

2 PETER 3:18 NASB

Knowledge is gained by learning; trust by doubt; skill by practice; and love by love.

THOMAS SZASZ

Speaking Words of Life

Joy is found in giving the right answer.

~ *Proverbs 15:23 NIrV*

One day Kim met her friend Joyce for lunch and listened as Joyce poured out her frustrations. The women had graduated on the same day from the same university, but Kim had nailed a job right away and Joyce had not.

"I've researched local companies, sent out my résumé, and gone on lots of interviews," Joyce told Kim. "But so far, nothing. Maybe I'm just not good enough. I feel like giving up."

Kim just listened at first, but soon she felt God leading her to provide words of encouragement. She gave Joyce a good, uplifting pep talk. The expression on Joyce's face soon convinced Kim that her sincere words were having the desired effect.

As the two friends parted after lunch, Kim thought about how powerful a little encouragement could be. She thanked God for helping her to encourage her friend, and she expressed her gratitude to God for all of the times he had sent someone to encourage her in the same way.

Your words are powerful tools in the hands of God. When you reach out to another person, speaking words of encouragement and caring, you are doing God's work. According to the Bible, "the tongue has the power of life and death" (Proverbs 18:21). What an awesome responsibility and privilege it is to use your words to lift up another person. Learn to choose your words carefully, and you will find yourself with plenty of opportunities to do just that.

TRY THIS: *Think of someone you know who needs encouragement. Send that person a short note or e-mail to express your support for him or her and to remind that individual of all the important things he or she has done in the past. Don't make this a one-time event, but repeat the notes frequently so that person continues to be encouraged.*

GOOD PEOPLE WILL BE REWARDED FOR WHAT THEY SAY.

PROVERBS 13:2 GNT

ENCOURAGE ONE ANOTHER AND BUILD EACH OTHER UP, JUST AS IN FACT YOU ARE DOING.

1 THESSALONIANS 5:11 NIV

A word of encouragement during a failure is worth more than an hour of praise after success.

AUTHOR UNKNOWN

101

Waiting Has Its Reward

It is better to be patient than to fight.

— *Proverbs* 16:32 NIrV

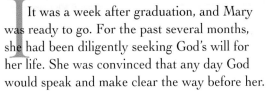

It was a week after graduation, and Mary was ready to go. For the past several months, she had been diligently seeking God's will for her life. She was convinced that any day God would speak and make clear the way before her.

"Any day now," she told God a few weeks later. "You can speak and tell me which way I need to go. I'm ready, willing, and waiting." But what she wasn't ready for was more waiting. It hadn't occurred to Mary that God would keep her in a holding pattern or that what God really wanted was for Mary to learn patience and let him set the agenda.

Mary finally decided to relax and trust God's timing. When she did, God provided her with wonderful opportunities in her own community—opportunities she might have missed if she had run off to find her own solution rather than waiting patiently on the Lord.

Patience as a virtue in today's fast-paced society of instant gratification is often overlooked. Patience is an important skill to learn, for it allows you to wait for the right opportunity to come along—the one that is in the center of God's plan for your life. Waiting patiently can be difficult, and it may take practice, but its sure rewards are peace and confidence.

Try this: One of the best ways to practice patience is by listening. In your conversations with others, make a point of really listening. Avoid planning what you are going to say next or interrupting with a story of your own. By doing this regularly and deliberately, you will discover that the more you practice patience, the easier it is for you to have.

WHOEVER IS SLOW TO ANGER HAS GREAT UNDERSTANDING, BUT ONE WHO HAS A HASTY TEMPER EXALTS FOLLY.

PROVERBS 14:29 NRSV

LIVE A LIFE WORTHY OF THE CALLING YOU HAVE RECEIVED. BE COMPLETELY HUMBLE AND GENTLE; BE PATIENT, BEARING WITH ONE ANOTHER IN LOVE.

EPHESIANS 4:1–2 NIV

The secret to patience is doing something else in the meanwhile.

AUTHOR UNKNOWN

PURPOSE

Each one of us does the work
which the Lord gave him to do:
I planted the seed,
Apollos watered the plant,
but it was God who made the plant grow . . .
God will reward each one according
to the work each has done.
For we are partners working
together for God.

I Corinthians 3:5–6, 8–9 GNT

The LORD has made everything for its purpose.

~ *Proverbs 16:4 NRSV*

We know that in all things God works for the good of those who love him, who have been called according to his purpose.

~ *Romans 8:28 NIV*

ORDINARY PEOPLE THINK MERELY OF SPENDING TIME. GREAT PEOPLE THINK OF USING IT.

AUTHOR UNKNOWN

Laughing It Up

A cheerful heart enjoys a good time that never ends.

~ *Proverbs 15:15 NIrV*

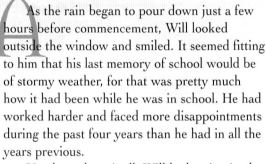

A GOOD LAUGH IS SUNSHINE IN A HOUSE.

WILLIAM MAKEPEACE THACKERAY

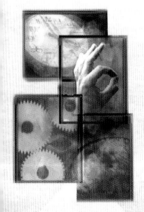

As the rain began to pour down just a few hours before commencement, Will looked outside the window and smiled. It seemed fitting to him that his last memory of school would be of stormy weather, for that was pretty much how it had been while he was in school. He had worked harder and faced more disappointments during the past four years than he had in all the years previous.

Yet throughout it all, Will had maintained his unfailing cheerful spirit. When others cracked under the pressure or quit, Will kept his head up and maintained his sense of humor. "Why not be happy?" he would often say to others. "God has done so much for me that I can't help but be cheerful."

And that day, Will was even more cheerful than usual, for he knew a bright, new challenge was ahead. He knew that God had done so much for him, and he was looking forward eagerly to what God had planned for his future.

Maintaining an attitude of cheerfulness is a decision—one you must make every day. It is choosing to keep yourself focused on the good things God has placed in your life. It is choosing to believe that God desires the best for you. It is choosing to believe that no matter what situations you encounter in this life, God will never leave your side. Choose every day to be cheerful.

Try this: Do something for yourself to increase your sense of personal cheerfulness. Take time to go to the amusement park, see a movie, or just hang out with friends. Reflect on some of the wonderful things God has placed in your life. And give God thanks for all his blessings to you.

Happiness is a choice that requires effort at times.

AUTHOR UNKNOWN

Safe from All Harm

God provides help and protection for those who are righteous and honest.

~ *Proverbs 2:7 GNT*

Rachel had grown up in a rural small town, and she wanted to attend a college in Chicago. When Rachel talked about it with her parents, though, she realized from her mom's furrowed brow that she certainly did not share her enthusiasm. Rachel's mom thought that big cities were dangerous, especially for young women Rachel's age.

"Oh, Mom," Rachel said, "I think I know what you're feeling, but it's time for me to face life on my own. You've taught me how to make good decisions that will keep me safe. I won't forget. But now it's time for you to trust in how you've raised me and, even more, to trust in God. He goes with me, you know. He's more than able to protect me."

Rachel's mom smiled and gave her a hug. "The best way for you to help me now," Rachel said, "is to pray for me every day and leave me in God's capable hands."

You can trust in God's protection. His resources are unlimited, and he never sleeps. Nonetheless, he expects his children to act responsibly. The book of Proverbs is filled with God's timeless wisdom for staying on the safe side of life. Proverbs points out the dangers along the path and urges you to keep your eyes open and your hand in the hand of God. Trust yourself to God—and do your part to live safely as well.

Try this: *During your quiet time this week, ask God specifically for his protection over you as you go about your daily tasks. Then choose a chapter from the book of Proverbs to read through. Use a highlighter to capture the nuggets of wisdom that stand out to you in the text.*

MY HEART TRUSTS IN THE LORD, AND I AM HELPED.

PSALM 28:7 NIV

THE LORD IS FAITHFUL, AND HE WILL STRENGTHEN YOU AND KEEP YOU SAFE FROM THE EVIL ONE.

2 THESSALONIANS 3:3 GNT

Happiness has many roots, but none more important than security.

E. R. STETTINIUS

Applying Your Skills

Do you see those who are skillful in their work? They will serve kings.

~ *Proverbs 22:29* NRSV

EVERY CALLING IS GREAT WHEN GREATLY PURSUED.

OLIVER WENDELL HOLMES

The young man thought that his career plans were all set. As the adopted son of a distinguished Egyptian family, he had received the best education available. Now that he had completed his studies, he would surely be in good standing for a cozy position in government.

However, God had another career in mind for the man—specifically, a career in leadership. Of course, when God told him about it, the man was doubtful he had the proper skills. "Who am I to lead anyone?" he questioned. "And what if they don't listen to me? Besides, I have this speech impediment."

Despite his hesitations, God reassured the man that he would provide all the skills necessary for him to be a great leader, and he even let him bring his brother, Aaron, along for moral support. So the man decided to trust God and take this new career one day at a time. And Moses became a mighty leader of the nation of Israel.

Once you actually get into your chosen field, you may discover that the career for which you have studied or trained is not quite what you expected. You may feel God leading you into an entirely different profession, which can feel uncomfortable, even scary. Always remember that when God puts a desire in your heart and you follow his plan, he will help you become equipped with the needed skills and abilities.

Try this: Write down a dozen or so things that you really love to do — things you get enthusiastic about. In another column list the careers that would be appropriate for your training and education. Now compare each list to determine if one has any relationship to the other. Ask God to lead you into a career you can really enjoy.

In his heart a man plans his course, but the Lord determines his steps.

PROVERBS 16:9 NIV

Whatever you do, work at it with all your heart, as though you were working for the Lord and not for people.

COLOSSIANS 3:23 GNT

Every job is a self-portrait of the person who did it. Autograph your work with excellence.

AUTHOR UNKNOWN

Why Wellness Matters

Do not be wise in your own eyes; fear the LORD and shun evil. This will bring health.

~ Proverbs 3:7–8 NIV

> CHEERFULNESS, SIR, IS THE PRINCIPLE INGREDIENT IN THE COMPOSITION OF HEALTH.
>
> ARTHUR MURPHY

Sue was often tempted to stay up late into the night socializing or studying, and she loved cream-filled sponge cakes and chocolate bars. She often substituted those, along with a diet cola, for the cafeteria food. She was usually too tired to exercise, but she told herself that she could always catch up when she had more time and the weather was a little bit better.

Right before Christmas break, she was feeling rundown and decided to check in with the school infirmary. "Maybe I'm doing too much," she told the nurse.

"More likely, you're not doing enough," the nurse responded, "and you weigh more than is healthy." She talked to Sue about getting adequate sleep, eating well, and exercising, and she gave Sue some written guidelines to lose some weight and stay in good shape.

Sue had grown up believing that her body was the temple of the Lord, as stated in 1 Corinthians 6:19. Now she was determined to honor God by taking good care of it.

As your life gets busier and busier after graduation, remember that God places great importance on good health. A basic commandment he gave to the Israelites in the Old Testament was to set aside one whole day for rest. God knows that when you push yourself too hard you increase your risk of illness. So take care of your body. Get enough rest, exercise, and eat right. Those habits will pay off throughout your life.

TRY THIS: For the next week, keep a record of your exercise, the food you eat, and the amount of sleep you get. Do you see any areas that need to be adjusted? Make a note of what needs to change. Is your weight within a healthy range? Are you getting a sufficient amount of sleep? Have any of your friends noticed a difference?

A CHEERFUL LOOK BRINGS JOY TO THE HEART, AND GOOD NEWS GIVES HEALTH TO THE BONES.

PROVERBS 15:30 NIV

I PRAY THAT IN ALL RESPECTS YOU MAY PROSPER AND BE IN GOOD HEALTH, JUST AS YOUR SOUL PROSPERS.

3 JOHN 1:2 NASB

He who enjoys good health is rich, though he knows it not.

ITALIAN PROVERB

POWER

The mighty power of God,
that made the mountains rise,
That spread the flowing seas abroad,
and built the lofty skies;
The wisdom that ordained
the sun to rule the day,
The moon shines full at God's command,
and all the stars obey.

Isaac Watts

A wise man has great power.

~ *Proverbs* 24:5 NIrV

Jesus said, "When the Holy Spirit comes upon you, you will be filled with power, and you will be witnesses for me in Jerusalem, in all of Judea and Samaria, and to the ends of the earth."

~ *Acts* 1:8 GNT

POWER IS NO BLESSING IN ITSELF, EXCEPT WHEN IT IS USED TO PROTECT THE INNOCENT.

JONATHAN SWIFT

ORDERING YOUR THOUGHTS

The LORD detests the thoughts of the wicked, but those of the pure are pleasing to him.

~ *Proverbs* 15:26 NIV

CHANGE YOUR THOUGHTS AND YOU CHANGE YOUR WORLD.

NORMAN VINCENT PEALE

Graduation was just a week away, and doubts filled Steve's mind. Could he earn the kind of money he needed? Did he have enough skills to succeed? Would anyone even bother to look at his résumé?

Steve's confidence began to crumple as these negative thoughts told hold in his mind. As he was praying one day, he felt God leading him to a passage in Philippians. "Whatsoever things are true . . ." he read, "whatsoever things are honest . . . whatsoever things are lovely . . . think on these things."

As soon as he read that, Steve grasped the application for his life. He hadn't been ordering his thoughts in the way that God wanted, for he had given priority to negative thoughts rather than positive ones. Steve began to consciously replace thoughts of doubt and indecision with thoughts of God's faithfulness and caring. His outlook on the future improved almost immediately, and he was soon pursuing new job leads with enthusiasm.

✺ Putting your thoughts in order is key. Your own thoughts affect you more than anyone else, and yet the thoughts that you choose to put into your head have a strong influence on others as well, because they govern the way you act in different situations. If you dwell on thoughts of failure and defeat, you could actually miss opportunities because you aren't looking for them. Make your thoughts work for you, and keep your mind open to fresh possibilities and new opportunities.

✺ Try this: *During the next few weeks, pick a passage in the Bible that you enjoy and spend five minutes each day going over each word and thinking about what it means to you. Meditate on your blessings and the gifts God has placed in your life. Think about the obstacles God has helped you overcome.*

The wisdom of the prudent is to give thought to their ways.

Proverbs 14:8 NIV

Search me, O God, and know my heart; test me and know my anxious thoughts. See if there is any offensive way in me, and lead me in the way everlasting.

Psalm 139:23–24 NIV

Do not think that what your thoughts dwell upon is of no matter. Your thoughts are making you.

Bishop Steere

What Comes First?

He who pursues righteousness and love finds life, prosperity and honor.

~ *Proverbs 21:21 NIV*

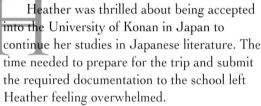

Seek first the good things of the mind, and the rest will either be supplied or its loss will not be felt.

Francis Bacon

Heather was thrilled about being accepted into the University of Konan in Japan to continue her studies in Japanese literature. The time needed to prepare for the trip and submit the required documentation to the school left Heather feeling overwhelmed.

Meeting the deadline became a top priority for Heather, and she found herself cutting short the time that she normally spent with friends, family and with God. In only a matter of days, she started feeling lonely, run down, and out of touch. Even though one of her professors suggested that she wait a year and put the paperwork on a more manageable time line, the trip remained her all-consuming priority.

Two weeks later, Heather's father had a light heart attack. He was back home the next day, but the thought that she could have lost her father helped Heather put things in perspective. Heather realized her personal relationships with her family, her friends, and God were more important than a trip that could wait for the next deadline.

✕ Something quite remarkable happens when you let God direct your priorities, and things start to fall into place. You're able to keep a clear head; you're able to balance the important (activities, trips, educational opportunities) with the vital (your relationship with God and your relationship with other people). When God directs your priorities, you feel more content knowing that God sees the big picture and is able to help you take advantage of worthwhile opportunities.

✕ TRY THIS: *Imagine for a moment that you suddenly got a great job in Europe, and you have one week left with your friends and family before you leave. Consider how you would spend that week and what things you would truly value. What insights into your values and priorities does this exercise give you?*

HONOR THE LORD BY MAKING HIM AN OFFERING FROM THE BEST OF ALL THAT YOUR LAND PRODUCES.

PROVERBS 3:9 GNT

JESUS SAID, "SEEK FIRST [YOUR HEAVENLY FATHER'S] KINGDOM AND HIS RIGHTEOUSNESS, AND ALL THESE THINGS WILL BE GIVEN TO YOU."

MATTHEW 6:33 NIV

It seems essential, in relationships and all tasks, that we concentrate only on what is more significant and important.

SÖREN KIERKEGAARD

A Life that Matters

The fruit that godly people bear is like a tree of life.

— *Proverbs* 11:30 NIrV

Doug and Grant were roommates during their senior year of college. Doug spent his last semester fretting about his plans after graduation. But when he talked to Grant about this, he marveled at how Grant seemed to be at peace no matter what. *I want that in my life*, he thought. He accepted Christ shortly thereafter, and when he graduated he began to attend a small church. There he met Mary, who would soon become his wife.

As Doug and Mary grew in their faith, they began to reach out to others, including a troubled teenager named Tim. With their encouragement, Tim gave his life to God, and several years later he traveled to Uganda to serve as a missionary. He brought the good news about God to thousands of people during his lifetime.

All of these wonderful events happened as the fruit of one seed planted by Doug's roommate, Grant, years earlier.

Living a righteous life for God is powerful. Be aware that the way you live your life will affect others. You may never know how something you do in a moment will affect someone for a lifetime, so be sure that you make your moments count. Live your life with the expectation that others are watching and learning from you. Above all, make sure that the seeds you plant in your community bear something beautiful and good.

TRY THIS: *For one day, make a conscious note of the types of things you say to others. At the end of the day, take some quiet time to evaluate the words you've said to others. Were they uplifting? Encouraging? Did they point others to God? Were they a true expression of your faith in God?*

THE FRUIT OF THE RIGHTEOUS IS A TREE OF LIFE, AND HE WHO WINS SOULS IS WISE.

PROVERBS 11:30 NIV

WE PRAY . . . THAT YOU MAY LIVE A LIFE WORTHY OF THE LORD AND MAY PLEASE HIM IN EVERY WAY: BEARING FRUIT IN EVERY GOOD WORK, GROWING IN THE KNOWLEDGE OF GOD.

COLOSSIANS 1:10 NIV

You have to sow before you can reap. You have to give before you can get.

ROBERT COLLIER

Always a Winner

It is the Lord who gives victory.

— *Proverbs 21:31* GNT

WITHOUT A STRUGGLE, THERE CAN BE NO PROGRESS.

FREDERICK DOUGLASS

Alissa knew that God had the power to give her the victory over any problem, issue, or struggle that came her way. But this situation seemed different, and Alissa was finding it hard to believe that she would have the victory.

After finally graduating from law school after six long years, Alissa believed she was ready to take the bar exam. But she failed miserably on the first try . . . and the second try . . . and the third try. Now she wondered if she had thrown away the last six years of her life.

Finally she cried out, "Lord, if this is your will for life, please let me pass this exam." She felt her burden lift from her shoulders, and a calming presence seemed to surround her. She began earnestly studying with renewed determination. When the fourth time came, she found she was able to concentrate on her weak points, study with more diligence, and pass the test.

God is willing and able to deliver you from any situation. You may ask, why does anyone have to struggle at all? Why doesn't God give instant victory? Part of the reason is that struggles teach you to depend upon him, for it is often only when you are completely in over your head that you realize you need God's help. If every situation came with an immediate resolution, you wouldn't learn to trust in God and submit to him.

Try this: *Read the story of David and Goliath in 1 Samuel 17, where, against all odds, God granted David an incredible victory. Pick out one area of your life where you have a struggle that seems daunting and give it to God in prayer. Look for the little victories that God gives you each day.*

THE LORD HOLDS VICTORY IN STORE FOR THE UPRIGHT.

PROVERBS 2:7 NIV

THANKS BE TO GOD, WHO GIVES US THE VICTORY THROUGH OUR LORD JESUS CHRIST.

1 CORINTHIANS 15:57 NASB

The way to grow strong in Christ is to become weak in yourself.

C. H. SPURGEON

LIFE

The only life that will endure,
Is one that's kind and good and pure;
And so for God I'll take my stand,
Each day I'll lend a helping hand,
I'll help someone in time of need,
And journey on with rapid speed.

William M. Golden

There is life in doing what is right. Along that path you will never die.

~ *Proverbs 12:28 NIrV*

God so loved the world that he gave his one and only Son, that whoever believes in him shall not perish but have eternal life.

~ *John 3:16 NIV*

LEARN FROM YESTERDAY, LIVE FOR TODAY, HOPE FOR TOMORROW.

AUTHOR UNKNOWN

At Inspirio we love to hear from you—your
stories, your feedback,
and your product ideas.
Please send your comments to us
by way of e-mail at
icares@zondervan.com
or to the address below:

inspirio

Attn: Inspirio Cares
5300 Patterson Avenue SE
Grand Rapids, MI 49530

If you would like further information
about Inspirio and the products we
create please visit us at:
www.inspiriogifts.com

Thank you and God Bless!